The
Painter's Plate

Teaching kids to discover their inner artistic ability by creating a masterpiece with food.

Written By: Emily Massey
Illustrated By: Angelina Hardin

Please let me introduce myself. My name is

Chef Seymour Nutrition.

I am what some people call a "magician in

the kitchen."

I would like to tell you a story, so you can understand, how I create culinary masterpieces with my very own two hands.

I wasn't always a magician in the kitchen. It used to be a chore, but then I discovered that I could do much more. Like creating plates of art with colors galore!

When I was just a young chef, pleasing my

clients was never easy to do.

They were never happy with my blanched

chicken covered in fondue or noodles alla

coo-coo.

They were not happy with my plain white rice; they told me it needed more color and spice.

"This is bland!"

"This is yucky!"

"This plate is boring!"

All of a sudden my boss came into the

kitchen with a frown.

He said, "You are making me lose money

and keeping my returning customer count

down!"

I was heartbroken, sad, embarrassed, and

mad!

My lifelong dream! How could I be so bad?

I ran out of the kitchen and into the street. I

kept running so fast I could barely see my

feet.

My heart was pounding, my breathing was

fast, and I was sweating from my forehead

all the way down to my underpants!

I had to slow down, perhaps get some water.

I looked up, and to my amazement I had run

so much farther!

I had made it downtown to the museum of

art. I thought to myself, *Surely there has to*

be a water fountain around these parts!

I entered the museum and stumbled upon a brand-new exhibit.
The art had eye-catching vibrant colors, movement, and texture. It was absolutely exquisite!

The featured work was Pablo Picasso's art. My thirst was forgotten because his paintings were so smart!

Masterpieces, I should say, he created paintings with colors galore. Yes, colors that make the eyes explore. One, two, three, and four, and many more colors from the ceiling to the floor.

Then in an instant it all became clear. I knew how to create culinary art with my very own two hands—just watch it appear.

I am going to create dishes that my customers are going to adore.
They are going to be running back to the restaurant begging for more.

I must get back to the kitchen and talk to my boss. I have the solution for no more customer loss.

Again, I began running so fast I could barely see my feet. My lungs were burning, my breathing was fast, my heart was going

beat, beat, beat.

I made it to the kitchen, and he looked at me with surprise. I said, "I need to talk to you. There is something I just realized."

He said, "Slow down and please explain!"

I said, "I have come up with many new ideas within my very own brain. I know how to win customers and how to make them stay. They'll want to come back to our restaurant each and every day."

I began to explain how my plate was my new painting canvas and how using all the different colors and textures of fruits and vegetables could make a chef an artist.

I then began to explain the colors further and how certain fruits and vegetables belong with each other.

I began with red and finished with black. I know I mentioned hundreds of fruits and vegetables, and he was finally getting the knack.

First I started with Red. . .

Fruit: Cherries, Red Pear, Persimmons, Strawberries, Raspberries, Papaya, Grapefruit, and Watermelon.

Vegetables: Tomatoes, Radishes, Red Bell Pepper, Chile Pepper, and Red Potatoes.

Then Blue and Purple. . .

Fruits: Blueberries, Grapes, Figs, Dragon Fruit, and Guava.

Vegetables: Eggplant, Purple Cabbage, Purple Onion, Purple Cauliflower, and Purple Fingerling Potatoes.

Then Green. . .

Fruit: Green Grapes, Green Apple, Kiwi Pear, Honeydew, and Lime.

Vegetables: Spinach, Artichoke, Arugula, Asparagus, Avocados, Broccoli, Brussel Sprouts, Chayote Squash, Bok Choy, Cucumbers, Green Beans, Green Onions, Green Peppers, Celery, Sugar Snap Peas, Okra, and Zucchini.

<u>And then White. . .</u>

Fruit: Bananas, Ginger, White Peaches, and White Nectarines.

Vegetables: Cauliflower, Garlic, Jicama, Mushrooms, Parsnips, and White Corn.

Then Yellow and Orange. . .

Fruit: Apricots, Cantaloupe, Pineapple, Peach, Tangerine, Mangos, Papaya, Lemon, Golden Kiwi, and Yellow Apple.

Vegetables: Sweet Potato, Yellow Peppers, Yellow Squash, Butternut Squash, Corn, Carrot, Spaghetti Squash, and Pumpkin.

And finally Black. . .

Fruit: Black Grapes and Blackberries

Vegetables: Black Olives and Eggplant.

You see, in the past, when my food

was not the best,

I did not know how to add color

with fruits and vegetables to give my dishes

some zest!

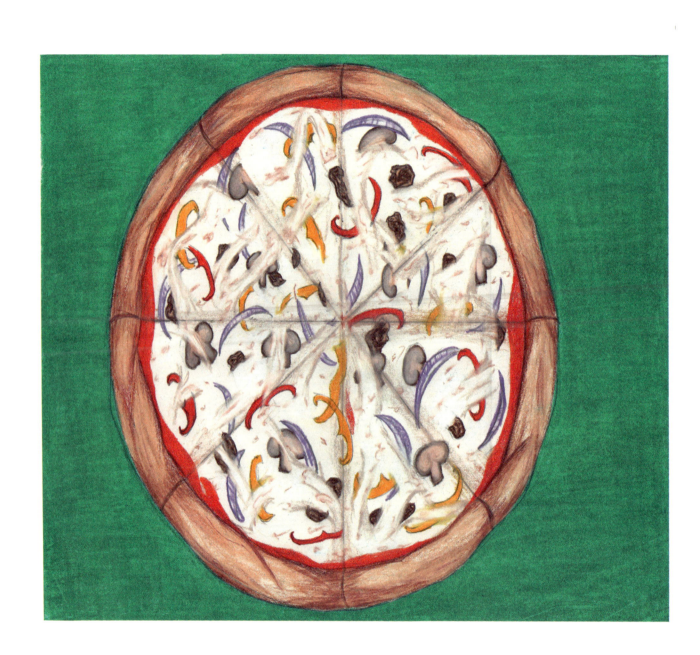

Now that I have explained the colors of foods, let us now put them together and create art with food!

So everyone, become your own artist and

grant me this wish, start adding some color

to your favorite dish!

Rainbow Oatmeal (2 servings)
Ingredients:
½ cup oatmeal
1 cup water
2 tbsp. peanut butter, sunflower butter, cashew or almond butter
2 tsp honey
¼ cup Blue-blueberries
¼ cup Red-strawberries
¼ cup White-bananas
¼ cup orange/yellow-peaches

Directions:
On the stove, heat the oatmeal and water in a pan until simmering and thickened (about 3 minutes). Add the nut butter or sunflower butter, stir to mix. Remove from heat and pour into a bowl. Top with a variety of fruit and drizzle with honey.

Beautiful Yogurt Parfait (4 servings)
Ingredients:
4 cups vanilla Greek yogurt (or any of your favorite flavors)
1 cup Blue-Blueberries
1 cup Black-Blackberries
1 cup Red-Raspberries
1 cup Orange/yellow-Mango, chopped
1 cup Green-Kiwi, sliced
1 cup walnuts (chopped) or sunflower seeds-Brown
½ cup dark chocolate chips-Black

Directions:
Begin layering the bottom of an individual glass with blueberries, then yogurt, then blackberries, then yogurt, then raspberries, then yogurt, then mango, then yogurt, then kiwi, then yogurt, then top with walnuts and dark chocolate chips. Now that is beautiful!

The Picasso Pasta Salad (cold pasta salad)
(6 servings)
Ingredients:
1 lb whole wheat rotini (or any shape pasta)
½ cup Orange bell peppers
¾ cup Red grape tomatoes
1 cup White-chopped cooked chicken and/or cubed fresh mozzarella cheese
¾ cup Green peas
½ cup Purple cabbage, chopped
2 tbsp. fresh basil-Green
1 tbsp. fresh oregano-Green
¼ cup shredded parmesan cheese

Directions:
Add water to a large stock pot. Add 1 tbsp. salt to your pasta water. Allow the water to come to a boil on high on the stove. Add the pasta. Cook until it has a tender texture but a firm bite (al dente). Allow pasta to cool. Pour cool pasta into a bowl and toss with all the colorful ingredients. Finish the pasta by drizzling the apple cider vinaigrette, toss, and top with fresh basil and parmesan cheese.

For the Apple Cider Vinaigrette:
½ cup apple cider vinegar
1 tbsp. Dijon mustard
1 shallot, chopped
1 garlic clove, chopped
2 tbsp. honey
Salt and pepper to taste

Directions:
Blend all ingredients except the oil until smooth. When smooth, add the oil in a steady stream into the mixture while blending at the same time.

The Painter's Palette Pizza
(Individual serving)

Ingredients:

1 whole wheat pita bread

¼ cup favorite marinara sauce

½ cup shredded part-skim mozzarella

2 tbsp. shredded parmesan cheese

3 strips Red- bell peppers, sliced

1 Brown- mushrooms, sliced

1 tbsp. Black- olives, sliced

¼ cup Green-broccoli, chopped

3 strips Orange-bell peppers, sliced

1 tsp Purple-onions chopped

Directions:

Preheat oven to 425 degrees. Place the pita on a baking sheet or pizza stone. Spread the marinara sauce on the pita bread.

Top with mozzarella and parmesan cheese. Finish by decorating the pizza with all the different colors of the toppings. Bake for 25 minutes.

Author: Emily Eckert Massey

Emily's love for food began as a young child cooking with her mom, who was always creating unique and healthy dishes in Camden, Arkansas. Studying at the University of Arkansas, Emily received a B.S. in Dietetics. Instead of taking the typical career path of a dietitian, Emily decided to further her knowledge of food by attending Florida Culinary Institute where she received a double degree in International Pastry and Culinary Arts. Her passion for cooking led her to create a personal chef business, Simply Scrumptious, LLC. She operated Simply Scrumptious, LLC in Palm Beach Gardens, Florida before moving to their home in Fayetteville, Arkansas where she lives with her husband, Jeff, and daughter, Kate. Her goal is to create beautiful dishes and to teach people how to make healthy and delicious foods by using all their senses.

Illustrator: Angelina Hardin

Angelina Hardin lives in Camden, Arkansas with her beautiful twin daughters, Taylor and Tyler. In the past, she served four years in the United States Air Force as a B-52 Crew Chief. Today, she starts her days entertaining students in a local public school system as a teacher, and continues in the evenings teaching gymnastics and aerobics. At the end of her day, she enjoys drawing, painting, and sculpting.